PLAYING to WIN

The Story of Althea Gibson

by **KAREN DEANS**

illustrated by **ELBRITE BROWN**

HOLIDAY HOUSE / NEW YORK

For my Mom and Dad,
whose passions in life have helped inspire my own. I love you.
K. D.

To William N. Brown III (my uncle)
During my childhood you would sit and draw pictures with me
and also bring me art supplies. You couldn't image how much this
meant to me! Thanks for always believing in me.

To Henrietta Smith from ALA
Every time I talk to you, you leave me inspired; you make me feel
like I can fly. Thanks for your encouragement.

To Mr. Frank Stephens—a retired art director from the main branch
of the Free Library of Philadelphia
When I was lost you always helped me find my way. I hope to make
a difference in the lives of young people the way you have made a
difference in my life.
E. B.

Text copyright © 2007 by Karen Deans | Illustrations copyright © 2007 by Elbrite Brown
| All Rights Reserved | Printed and Bound in China
The typeface is Agenda. The illustrations were done in acrylic paint, pencil, cut and torn
paper, Caran d'Ache crayon, and cardboard attached to 300 lb., watercolor paper. Some
pieces were coated with gesso.
www.holidayhouse.com | First Edition | 1 3 5 7 9 10 8 6 4 2

Library of Congress Cataloging-in-Publication Data
Deans, Karen.
Playing to win : the story of Althea Gibson / by Karen Deans ;
illustrated by Elbrite Brown.— 1st ed.
p. cm.
Includes bibliographical references.
ISBN 0-8234-1926-6 (hardcover)
1. Gibson, Althea, 1927—Juvenile literature. 2. Tennis players—United States—
Biography—Juvenile literature. 3. African American women tennis players—Biography—
Juvenile literature. I. Brown, Elbrite II. Title.

GV994.G53D43 2007   ISBN-13: 978-0-8234-1926-5
796.342'092—dc22   ISBN-10: 0-8234-1926-6
2004052275

Designed by Yvette Lenhart

When Althea Gibson was born on August 25, 1927, few would have imagined she was destined for greatness. She was the first child of poor sharecroppers living in South Carolina. Her parents, Annie and Daniel, worked hard, trying to scratch out a living on a cotton farm. Each summer they raised five acres of cotton in exchange for a place to live, which was nothing more than a small wooden cabin. As sharecroppers, they were given part of the cotton they farmed. They sold it to buy just enough food and clothing to get by on.

Times were not good for the Gibson family; so when Althea was three, her parents sent her up North to live with her Aunt Sally, hoping things might improve for her there. Unfortunately, things weren't much better in New York City, so she was sent to live with her Aunt Daisy in Philadelphia. Finally, when Althea was nine, her parents moved to New York and the family settled into an apartment in Harlem. At last Althea was together with her parents, her three little sisters, and her brother.

In the 1930s life in Harlem was tough on kids trying to grow up. Crime was everywhere, and people were poor. Althea was becoming wild. She was either fighting with other kids or skipping school. Sometimes Althea, who loved movies, would play hooky all day in the movie theater. No matter how hard her parents tried, they couldn't keep Althea in line. She had a restless, determined nature that hadn't found a good way to express itself yet.

When she was thirteen, Althea realized she loved to play ball, any kind of ball. Instead of fighting, she started bowling and playing basketball and paddle tennis. She found she was happiest when she was competing in sports, and she was good at just about anything she tried. When she was fourteen years old, a grown-up friend named Buddy Walker recognized how talented she was at paddle tennis and thought she would be good at real tennis. He bought her a used tennis racket, and sure enough, she was a natural!

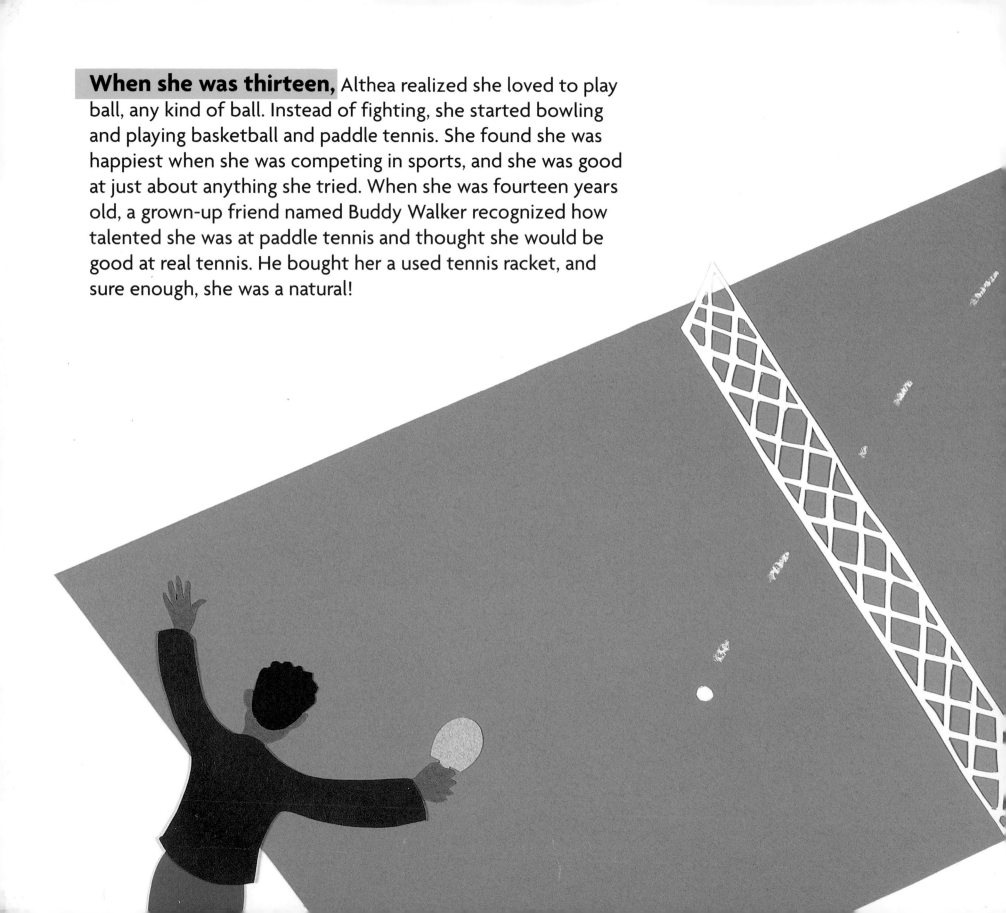

During the 1940s, tennis was a game played mostly by wealthy white people. The country clubs that had tennis courts would not let black people play. Fortunately for Althea, there was a tennis club for African Americans in New York called the Cosmopolitan Club. It was there that Althea began playing tennis, entering tournaments, and winning matches. But even when she was having success on the tennis court, she was still having trouble at school. She felt that it was a waste of time — she wanted to play tennis instead.

And play tennis she did. There was an African American tennis league called the American Tennis Association (ATA) that held tournaments throughout the year. In 1947, at the age of twenty, Althea won ten straight tournaments in the ATA. She was a champion in the black tennis community, and people were taking notice of her talent. Althea wanted more competition, though. She dreamed of playing in the famous

United States Lawn Tennis Association (USLTA). The only problem was, the officials made it difficult for African Americans to participate. While African Americans were not banned from the league, the championship matches were held at country clubs where they were not allowed. Only one black person, Reginald Weir, had ever entered a USLTA event before. He had lost after the second round.

Luckily there were people who wanted to see Althea succeed. One friend, Dr. Hubert Eaton, invited her to live in his family's home in North Carolina, where she could finish high school, as well as play tennis on his private court. While Althea appreciated his kindness and help, it was difficult for her to live in the South. In North Carolina she was forced to sit in the back of the bus because of her skin color. In those days black people were discriminated against openly in the South, and this made Althea feel terrible.

Though she longed to be in the North again, Althea went to college at Florida A&M, an all-black college where she was offered a scholarship to play tennis. There she began competing in tournaments against white players. In 1950 she qualified to play in the U.S. National Tennis Championships at Forest Hills, the most important USLTA tennis tournament in the United States. Althea was the first African American allowed to play there.

She became a curiosity to many spectators and officials. Some objected to her participation and doubted that she was any good. She gave them something to notice. In her second-round match against a top-ranked player, Althea was headed for victory when suddenly dark clouds covered the sky. Thunder rumbled over the sounds of bouncing tennis balls, and lightning struck down on Forest Hills. Officials stopped the game. When it resumed the next day, Althea lost. But she had broken down a barrier: people were taking her seriously. She was a contender.

During the next few years, Althea struggled. She continued to play in tournaments but did not do well. Some newspapers wrote that she was a big disappointment. Her supporters in the African American community were losing hope that she would ever be number one. Pretty soon she started losing confidence in her game. At one point she was so discouraged, she almost quit playing tennis to join the army. A good friend, Sydney Llewellyn, a taxi driver and tennis coach, convinced her to keep playing. He believed she could be the best in the game, so he coached her and encouraged her to play like a champion.

In 1955 the U.S. government asked Althea to become a goodwill ambassador as part of a traveling tennis team. The team of two men and two women journeyed around the world playing tennis. It was the best thing that could have happened for Althea's career. It allowed her to play lots of tennis while touring Southeast Asia. She saw many sights, met people, had fun, and improved her game.

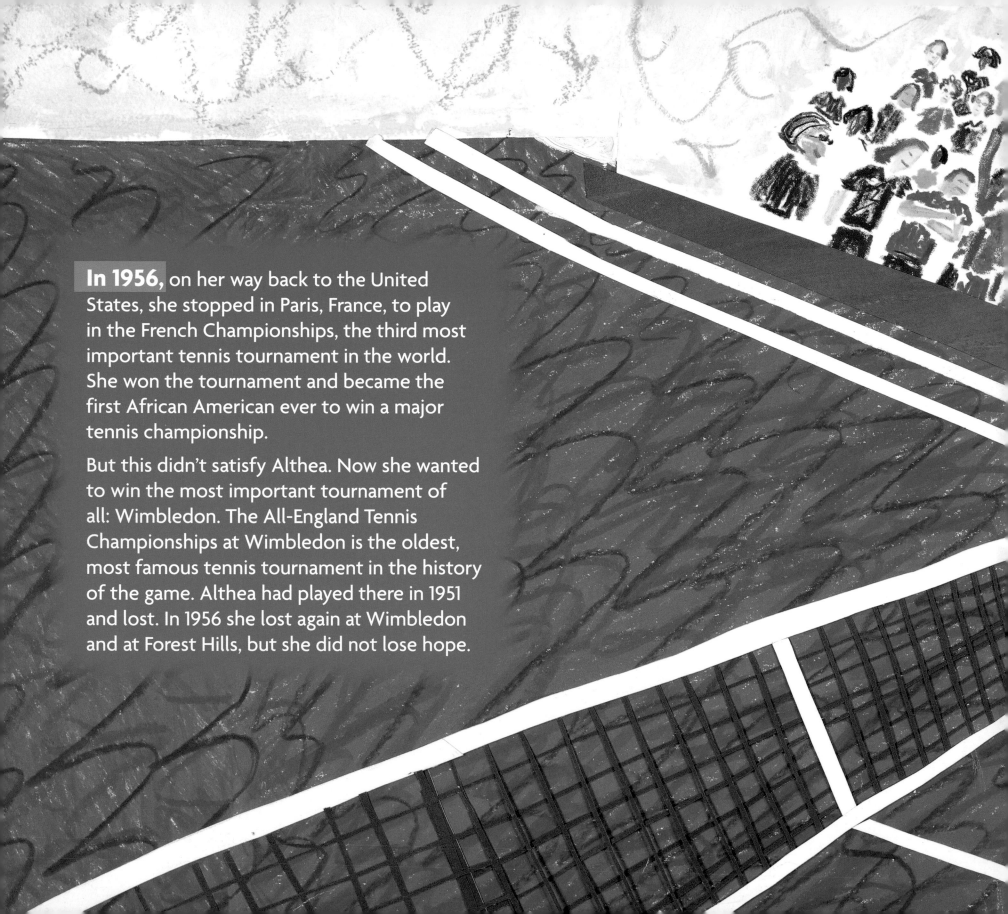

In 1956, on her way back to the United States, she stopped in Paris, France, to play in the French Championships, the third most important tennis tournament in the world. She won the tournament and became the first African American ever to win a major tennis championship.

But this didn't satisfy Althea. Now she wanted to win the most important tournament of all: Wimbledon. The All-England Tennis Championships at Wimbledon is the oldest, most famous tennis tournament in the history of the game. Althea had played there in 1951 and lost. In 1956 she lost again at Wimbledon and at Forest Hills, but she did not lose hope.

Althea had gone further than any African American tennis player in history, but she didn't believe she had gone far enough. She wanted to be number one in the world. She had the physical skill, but something was holding her back. She continued to play that year, traveling to Australia and Asia for a series of tournaments. She wasn't winning the way she wanted to, however; and on her return to the States, she decided it was time for her to win at Wimbledon and Forest Hills. In 1957 she was going to make it happen.

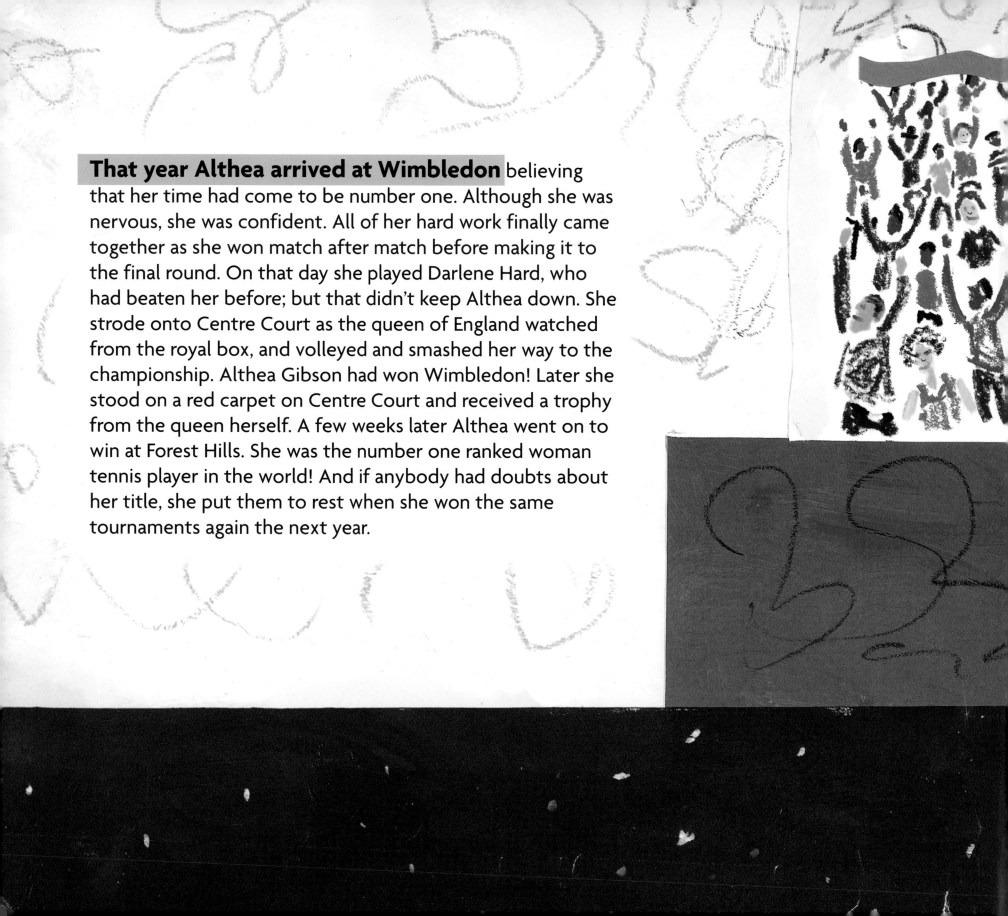

That year Althea arrived at Wimbledon believing that her time had come to be number one. Although she was nervous, she was confident. All of her hard work finally came together as she won match after match before making it to the final round. On that day she played Darlene Hard, who had beaten her before; but that didn't keep Althea down. She strode onto Centre Court as the queen of England watched from the royal box, and volleyed and smashed her way to the championship. Althea Gibson had won Wimbledon! Later she stood on a red carpet on Centre Court and received a trophy from the queen herself. A few weeks later Althea went on to win at Forest Hills. She was the number one ranked woman tennis player in the world! And if anybody had doubts about her title, she put them to rest when she won the same tournaments again the next year.

Althea Gibson loved to play tennis. She became number one by playing hard and never giving up, even during the tough times. She gladly accepted the help of supportive friends and graciously acknowledged their contributions to her career. Whatever Althea did to break down racial barriers in tennis, she did the only way she knew how: she played tennis like nobody's business.

Author's Note

Not only was Althea Gibson a champion on the tennis court, she was a talented singer and performed twice on *The Ed Sullivan Show*. She also acted in a movie starring John Wayne. In her thirties she took up golf and became the first African American to play professionally for the Ladies Professional Golf Association (LPGA). In her later years she devoted her life to helping children pursue their dreams of playing tennis and golf. She created The Althea Gibson Foundation for this purpose.

Important Dates

1927	Born in Silver, South Carolina, on August 25.
1941	Took tennis lessons at Harlem's Cosmopolitan Club.
1942	Won her first tournament sponsored by the American Tennis Association (ATA), an all-black organization.
1949	Played against white players for the first time.
1950	Competed in the U.S. National Tennis Championships at Forest Hills.
1951	Entered the All-England Tennis Championships at Wimbledon.
1953	Graduated from Florida A&M.
1955–56	Played tennis throughout Southeast Asia as a goodwill ambassador.
1956	Won the French Championships.
1957	Won at Wimbledon and Forest Hills.
1958	Duplicated her wins at Wimbledon and Forest Hills.
1959	Appeared in a film and released a record album.
1964	Began a professional golf career, joining the Ladies Professional Golf Association (LPGA).
1971	Ended golf career; became a professional tennis teacher.
2003	Died in East Orange, New Jersey, on September 28.

Selected Bibliography and Further Readings

Biracree, Tom. *Althea Gibson: Tennis Champion*. Los Angeles: Melrose Square Publishing Company, 1990.

Davidson, Sue. *Changing the Game: The Stories of Tennis Champions Alice Marble & Althea Gibson*. Seattle: Seal Press, 1997.

Gibson, Althea. *I Always Wanted to Be Somebody*. New York: Harper and Brothers, 1958.

Gibson, Althea, with Richard Curtis. *So Much to Live For*. New York: Putnam, 1968.

Gray, Frances Clayton, and Yanick Rice Lamb. *Born to Win: The Authorized Biography of Althea Gibson*. Hoboken, NJ: John Wiley & Sons, 2004.

Learn more about Althea on the web

www.altheagibson.com

www.tennisfame.org

www.womenshistory.about.com/od/gibsonalthea/a/althea_gibson.htm